What's
Dad
thinkin'?

What's Dad thinkin'?

A lighthearted look at our Family Tree
by David Butler

Andrews McMeel Publishing

Kansas City

There is a funny beast that roams my household.

We call him Dad.

He meanders about the hallways and corridors of our world like he owns the joint, confident in his capacity to rule. He's the guy to go to when someone in the pack is in need of a kind word, or some sense of direction.

He's probably not so different from your dad.
He makes funny noises, says strange things, and
swaggers about his domain trying to look busy—
until Mom tells him to do something.

He can make the heavens fall with just a glare, but would rather make us laugh till we ache with the simplest gesture or surprising breach of character.

Of course, no two dads are alike.

But there are certain "Dadisms" that
seem to transcend the boundaries of culture,
race, and geography. Like that furrowed brow
and squinting eye that seems to indicate

"I don't have a
clue what's going on,
but everything is
under control."

And that's the thing with Dad.

It's all about the illusion of control. As long as he figures things are going according to his skillfully composed master plan there isn't a problem in the world! And that's the way we like it.

One thing's for sure, Dad is a complex guy.
He seems to know how everything works
but can't always fix things that break.

"Planned obsolescence," he'll say.

He waters and feeds the grass and then
moans when he has to cut it.

He gets a big fire going on the grill
and then has to throw water on it.

He's funny to watch.

Nobody ever questions Dad while he's doing
stuff, but we all wonder,

"What's Dad thinkin'?"

He's a big walking riddle.

We figure if we can fit any two pieces of
the jigsaw of Dad together, we might be able
to figure out what makes him tick. But we just can't
seem to do it. Yet we know him sooo well.

Except for a few minor mysteries.

Dad goes off to work every day but none
of us really know what he does. We think he's either a
physicist or a toaster salesman.

We can't ever get a straight answer out of him.

For the longest time I thought Dad was
an astronaut. Then I asked him how big the
universe was. He spread his arms wide and said,

"Really big."

I'm pretty sure he's a toaster salesman.

Although he must be a fairly important guy because he comes home every day and exclaims

"You wouldn't believe the day I had!"

And then proceeds not to tell us. I guess if we wouldn't believe it, it must be pretty epic.

I know one thing, when he was young things were different. He had to walk farther, work longer for less money, handle dangerous equipment, and, occasionally, achieve feats of physical prowess that we still find very hard to believe.

He also volunteers a great deal of information about his "antics" as a youth. He assumes that these stories will dissuade us from creating mischief and getting in trouble, but we find them very inspiring. Especially since he laughs when he recounts them.

Apparently Mom took part in a
few of those stories.

But he never gets to finish those.

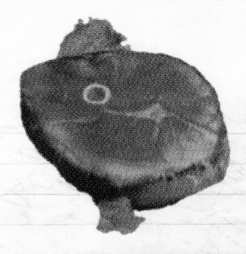

It seems that Dad didn't get much to eat as a youth either, considering how he will eat almost anything that is laid out in front of him now. He consumes frightening combinations of food, at frightening speed. I dare not spill ketchup on my hand at the table in fear of accidentally losing a finger. We sit in awe of such raw talent and fortitude.

Dad's great about showing us how to do stuff.

Even if he doesn't really know what he's doing, he passes that knowledge on to us.

Sometimes we learn how to really do it in school, but it's never as much fun.

His capacity to understand the nuances of particular sports is staggering, and his knowledge of history and political science is apparently boundless.

Yet he lacks the ability to match socks.

He knows so much about so many things, but never seems to know what's going on around him. He can fill you in on the latest stock info or a big trade in the NFL, but didn't know that the slumber party was going down tonight in his den or that a giant fountain of steaming hot water was billowing from the kitchen wall.

Like the eye of a hurricane, Dad remains composed while all heck breaks loose around him.

That is, of course, until he gets hit by the debris.

That's when we see Dad on the "edge."

The seas part to allow our benevolent dictator room to
vent, to recompose, and then to
disappear into Zen meditation with a swell
magazine or some goofy new gadget.

He'll usually get the "edge" while driving, too.
It has become apparent to us all that Dad is the only
person alive that knows how to drive a car.
Because he tells us so.

He has a full understanding of the laws and is able to
direct traffic, dictate specifics from the driver's
manual to the less enlightened, steer, shift, eat,
drink, brake, and swear, all within the confines of his
seat belt. But when someone in another car is talking
on their cell phone while driving, it makes him crazy!

Oh, and driving is a privilege, not a right.

But never, never ask Dad to get out the map.
He knows where he's going.

This is a shortcut.

And remember, "It's not too late to turn this car
around and head right back home."

I wouldn't ask Dad about his "style" or fashion sense either. He moves in circles where fashion is dictated by function or by team spirit.

Remember that bright, shiny new bike of yours?

He didn't make the money to buy it on the runways of Paris. Let's leave it at that!

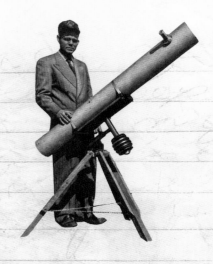

Dad doesn't have to be trendy.

Just look at him!

Trends are for sheep. And Dad's been cutting
his own path his entire life.

That's way cooler than any trend.

The whole "dad" aesthetic is that of timeless comfort and ease. So when he gets out of his workaday getup and slips into dad mode, you'll understand why he looks like a really big fifth-grader.

Now, about those brown loafers. . .

That's one of the best things about Dad.
He makes you see that you don't ever have
to stop being a kid at heart.

You can just become a big kid with big toys.

GO... GO...

EV...
wi...
C...

50 miles per
75 miles per g

OCT 1965

And take big naps.

Long naps.

Hibernation naps.

Sleeping becomes a hobby when you're a dad. He has to literally sneak away to make time for it.

He devotes so much of his time to us and to work, so we try to give him time to explore all his other interests.

Most of which are pretty weird.

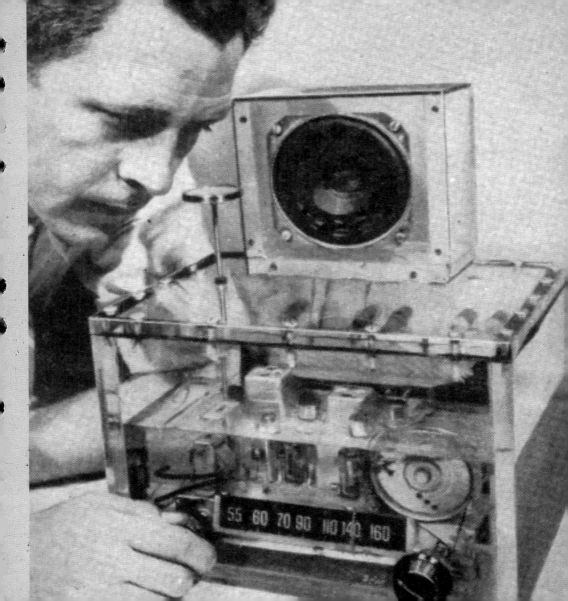

Dad's really into his hobbies. Some dads live in workshops or garages or dens, but my dad lives in the basement with his new train set. A while back it was steam engines, then it was race cars, beer can collecting, and fancy cigars!

All of these got on Mom's nerves.

Maybe she won't mind his conductor's hat and new steam whistle!

The best thing about Dad's hobbies?

They open our worlds up to many different ideas and creative ventures. They give us time to share with Dad, and figure out how to solve problems and think independently.

But most of all, they scare us.

And hardly anything is more confusing
than a dad lineup.

You thought your dad was a tough nut to
crack, what about all the other dads in
the neighborhood?

It's funny when Dad hangs around other dads. They all
stand around whispering and laughing with their hands
in their pockets like kids on the playground. Looking
around like they're about to get in trouble. They act
like the moms don't know what they're doing.

SPEAK
NO EVIL

SEE
NO EVIL

HEAR
NO EVIL

PAT.APLD.

Most of the time Dad sets a pretty good example, but when he gets together with friends he seems a little mischievous.

They call him "the instigator."

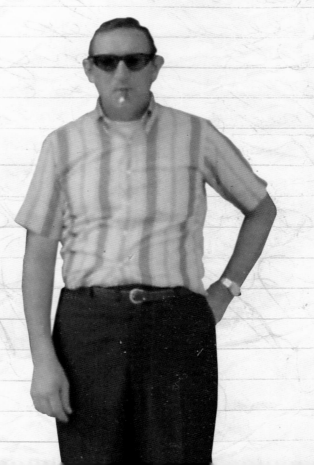

To relax on the weekends he goes out golfing.

He gets up early and is truly happy, with his big wad
of cash and fresh box of golf balls.

He usually comes home at dinnertime, cranky with a
headache and some stories about how he needs new
clubs and spent the day in the sand.

He says it calms his nerves.

But he never gets flustered when showing us how
to play. He seems to know a little bit about
everything. How to throw, how to hit, how to catch,
and how compassion and fair play are the most
important aspects of any game. Even when the world
seems otherwise interested in the glory and the glitz
of spectacle.

And in this way, Dad is a lighthouse in an occasionally unsettling sea. There is comfort in his consistency and nature—from years of finding his way, he has seen the roughest tides. Sure he seems salty, but that's the face he shows the world, to let them know he has made it despite the odds. And we are a testament to his loyalty.

You know why I love my dad? 'Cause no sacrifice is too great for his family. Just to make us laugh, he'd give up his own dignity. And that's the only thing important enough to him for such a sacrifice. Within the family, nothing is as important as being together.

And together, under his guidance, we've built up a family, like so many other projects that Dad has tackled. Nothing is as enviable as the strength of character that he has built up around him.

I will take up hammer and nails alongside my dad any time. And it will be the best thing that I can do, no matter how small the task. Because it will be done with him.

I think I know what Dad's thinkin'.

He loves us.

First published by MQ Publications Limited
12 The Ivories, 6-8 Northampton Street,
London N1 2HY

Copyright © 2002 by MQ Publications Limited
Text copyright © 2002 by David Butler
Design by Art of the Midwest Studio

ISBN 0-7407-2274-3

Library of Congress Control Number: 2001095904

Printed and bound in China